Love Until it Hurts

D1390522

To

The poorest of the poor – the lonely and the un-
loved. For it is by giving that one receives, it is by
forgetting oneself that one finds oneself.

Love Until it Hurts

Daphne Rae

HODDER AND STOUGHTON
LONDON SYDNEY AUCKLAND TORONTO

Introduction

Daphne Rae was born in Ceylon in 1933. Her father was one of that vast army of ex-patriate British who ran the administrative and commercial life of the Empire. When Daphne was five her father died suddenly and she started a long trail through some of the less-well-run boarding schools of England and Scotland. Her mother went out East again and remarried. The war started. Daphne became, in effect, an orphan, not knowing where the school holidays would be spent, treated with great kindness by the parents of one of her school friends and with intermittent cruelty by a sadistic great-uncle. When the war ended she was sent alone to Lymm station in Cheshire to meet the train on which her mother was travelling from London. She had a photograph of her mother in her hand as she stood beside the ticket collector. A woman approached. They exchanged glances. The woman walked past and got into a waiting car. Mother and daughter had failed to recognise one another.

Daphne remained at boarding school in Scotland until she was sixteen. Three factors had enabled her to overcome the loneliness of her childhood: her Christian faith, her determination to qualify as a doctor and the warm welcome she had always received from the family of her school friend – Jane Darlington. Her ambition to become a doctor was thwarted by a limitation typical of girls' schools at that time and for long after: there was no science teaching other than a ramble through the more ladylike aspects of biology. Without qualifications there was no chance of entry to medical school. Her mother returned to the East and took Daphne with her. For three years, in Singapore and Bankok, Daphne tried without success to find a way of studying for those elusive qualifications. When she was nineteen she returned to England, staying with friends and knocking without response on the doors of medical schools. Eventually she went to Cambridge, found digs, worked as a waitress to pay the rent and enrolled at the Technical College for A-levels in Science. This time it was marriage that intervened.

For the next twenty-three years her life was her family. She had six children, four daughters and then unidentical twin sons. Her marriage, like most marriages, had its joys and difficulties, its moments of happiness and frustration. She moved – inevitably it seems in retrospect – towards the Roman Catholic Church. The help and support she received from family friends such as the Jesuit, Father Tom Corbishley, the parish priest, Father Ronald MacDonald and a Benedictine Abbot, guided her to her conversion in 1977. The new Archbishop of Westminster, Father Basil Hume, encouraged her to do a post-graduate Diploma of Pastoral Theology with the Jesuits at Heythrop College in the University of London. It was not medicine but it paved the way for a new departure in her life; if she could not be a doctor she could nevertheless use the insights of her faith and her gift for understanding the nature of suffering. For two years she worked part-time at a home for the terminally ill and dying.

But part-time work was not enough. There is a time in the evolution of marriage – youngest children growing up, husbands preoccupied with their careers – when some women turn to coffee mornings and good works. Daphne could never have accepted that role. She wanted both to give herself fully and to go where she was needed. The East drew her back.

In 1979, she wrote to the Sisters of Charity in Calcutta but received no reply. Mother Teresa is not concerned with correspondence: if people really want to work with the Sisters, they will come. In September 1979, Daphne went to Heathrow Airport and got on a flight to India. It was the start of an experience that at long last fulfilled her childhood ambition to work with the sick and suffering. She has made two long visits to India and plans to go again in the Autumn of 1980. After that she may work with the Sisters of Charity anywhere but it is with India that she feels a special relationship. Like so many British men and women in the past she has experienced in India the paradox of belonging in a foreign land.

To those critics – and they exist – who say that charity begins at home, Daphne would reply that anywhere she feels needed *is* home. And she would perhaps echo Mahatma Gandhi: "There is no limit to extending our services to our neighbours across State-made frontiers. God never made those frontiers."

India has not made Daphne a different person but it has made her a more fulfilled person. In a way that is difficult to explain, it has also made her family both more fulfilled and happier.

Daphne is my wife.

April 1980

5

Contents

I am indebted to my dear friends Minos and Katingo. It was
they who sent me my first ticket to India. And to Bruce and
Sally who gave me the freedom of their house. Through their
love, I am learning to understand how to give – and accept –
love. Thank you.

1

Write...

"Write, for if your writing should make anyone more aware of God and their neighbour, then you must write," so said Mother Teresa, and this duty was confirmed by the publisher.

This is a book of the present and the future – a book which had its beginning when Mother Teresa left the Loretto nuns with five rupees in her pocket to fulfil her decision to walk alone with God and work among the poorest of the poor in the slums of Calcutta. It is a book about the faith and love which have matured and now saturate a large community of devoted men and women who are the Missionaries of Charity.

In a world that is increasingly in conflict, modern day pressures make us withdraw into ourselves. The purpose of life is made even more mysterious through war, hatred and greed, and the poor become victims of injustice. There are many who philosophise, who try to forget when we see posters of starving, disease-ridden children of the Third World. We try to forget that there are millions who are dying of starvation, T.B., leprosy and all the diseases that result from malnutrition. When we realise the truth, we are afraid because the problem is too big.

Mother Teresa was not afraid, even though she knew the enormity. She just went ahead in faith and did what was immediately in front of her. The Missionaries of Charity, too, have no fear – through their faith in God, they grow in strength and love. St. James said, "Show me your faith apart from your works, and I by my works will show you my faith" (James 2:18). Throughout the world, the nuns and brothers of the Missionaries of Charity, together with their helpers from every country are finding the truth in this – that their deeds lead to faith and to a direct experience of God in their souls.

What is it that makes the world award the Nobel Prize to Mother Teresa and her Missionaries? She is the epitome of the Order she founded, and she is respected and revered by people of all faiths. She has spirit and determination, she faces the problems of life, and acts on what she sees. "Wherever there is need among the poor and destitute in India, Australia, the Middle East or anywhere else in the world, I will set up a home and send my nuns or brothers." They work with the destitute and dying, the mentally handicapped, the alcoholics, the drug addicts, aborted and abandoned babies. God is supplying young men and women to the Order: at present there are ninety aspirants and three hundred and forty novices in the Mother House in Calcutta, and there is a constant stream of vocations both there and to the other Mother Houses of the Order. Men and women come as they know that God demands "their all", and they give their all willingly with love and joy. The vows of poverty, obedience and chastity are strengthened by the

Missionaries' special fourth vow of serving the poorest of the poor. As they say, "It is easy for us to do this, as our giving is voluntary. We live in the slums because we wish to, the poorest of the poor are forced to do so, and it is by serving them that we serve Christ."

It takes nine years before a sister or brother can take their final vows, and at any time during this period he or she can leave, or be asked to leave the Order. "Our aspirants spend six months with us before they become postulants, and a further six months before they become novices." (The brothers call their aspirants "Come and see's", continuing the invitation to the early disciples.) "After two years they take their first vows, and repeat this every year until their final vows." The aspirants, postulants and novices do exactly the same type of work as the professed Missionaries, but most of their time is spent in studying and in prayer. English is the common tongue, as the Missionaries come from all over the world. The majority come from India, but there are so many Indian languages, that it is impossible to learn them all.

Most of the novices enter the community when they are young, but their ages range from sixteen to sixty. The Mother House in Calcutta is bursting at the seams – "I am sleeping on the table tonight," said an Italian sister laughing, "we change every month, and last month I was in a bed, but we have so many sisters living here that we have to sleep in the refectory, on the tables, on the benches and on the floor. I sleep very well." Mother Teresa firmly believes that all the novices in India should have the privilege of living in the Mother House, and therefore at the heart of the Order.

Mother's original intention of working with the poorest of the poor was that she should live exactly as they do. She planned a diet of rice and salt – the poorest food of all – but the medical missionaries with whom she was training persuaded her that this would be morally wrong. If the nuns were to give their all, it was her responsibility to see that they should have a diet to enable them to fulfil this. Mother accepted the advice, and the food, although simple, is nutritious and adequate in amount.

Mother's constant thought is for the poorest of the poor. She will have nothing that looks too Western. An example of that concern occurred when I met the architect who was designing a new home being built in North India. He was anxious to use metal window frames instead of the more expensive wooden ones which are rapidly attacked by white ants. Sister Dorothy was certain that Mother would not approve as the metal frames would make the house appear too bright and expensive to the very poor, and so make them afraid to bring to the Missionaries those who are ill and who are in need.

2

Shishu Bhavan

Wherever the Missionaries of Charity work, they try to set up a *Nirmal Hriday*, a home for the destitute and dying, and a *Shishu Bhavan*, a home for all unwanted babies and children in need.

In Calcutta, Shishu Bhavan is two minutes' walk from Mother House — it is rapidly expanding and the Missionaries of Charity have acquired the house next door. This was much needed as the original Shishu Bhavan was bursting at the seams with activity. Sister Mongola is in charge of the older children. "It is sometimes heartbreaking when a number of children leave for adoption — I miss them so much, and yet I know that they will be happy," she says. When a child is sent to Europe, where there is a waiting list of prospective adopters, he is given a bag of beautiful clothing including winter woollens. In the bag is a card from those who have loved and cared for him.

Sammy, aged fifteen, is one who will probably not be adopted; he sits in a wheelchair, his withered body wasted by polio. He is "host" of the floor, always smiling and happy. Then there is another boy who is deaf but tries to make himself understood verbally. He is highly intelligent and top of his form, and at the age of seven understands English and Bengali. "I want to be adopted too," he says, "I would like to go to Europe by air" — all this in a mixture of sign language and written English. The family who will eventually adopt him will be blessed, for he is a delight.

Sister Shirley has an overcrowded ward for children of all ages. She is also surrounded by children who have been brought to day clinics. Some are tiny, weighing only a few pounds, and so weak through malnutrition that they can hardly hold themselves up — yet some of these are four or five years old. They often arrive too ill to save — it is heartbreaking for her. She is utterly devoted and rarely leaves them. It is amazing to watch her finding a tiny vein and setting up a life-saving drip. She has to cope with so many infections in her children — meningitis, dysentery, T.B., encephalitis, malaria and all the diseases resulting from malnutrition.

It is wonderful to bring a minute, aborted baby, weighing one and a quarter pounds and fighting for life, to Sister Teresina's premature ward, and to see the love and care where all the nuns on the ward join in the fight for life. "There are no incubators here, but the climate is kind to us. If we have a three-pound babe brought to us, then we are more confident over its future."

Fifty per cent of the smaller babies survive, and those that die have been loved and prayed for during their brief existence. The ones that live are wrapped in colourful blankets, often knitted by friends and co-workers all over the world. They wear tiny bonnets – so small that they must have been knitted from dolls patterns. These children grow up to be adopted – the boys in particular going to childless Indian families. It is hard for an Indian woman in a childless marriage to cope with the insults which she may have to contend with, and so husbands and wives go away for a few weeks, and return with a very small, but healthy baby from the premature ward of a Shishu Bhavan. "And matters are so arranged that no-one in the family knows that it is not their own. So a long desired child will be brought up as Hindu or Muslim in a happy family," said Sister Dionysia who painstakingly arranges the adoptions, and vets the prospective parents very carefully.

This ward also has its heartaches. Some abandoned premature babies arrive, perhaps surgically aborted after previous attempts by the mother to abort by taking pills. These babies are often large enough to appear to have a good chance of survival and then they suddenly turn blue and die from defects due to the abortive pills. "The world has given me the Nobel Prize," said Mother, "but I ask the world for a gift – I want the abortion laws abolished. This would be a real gift."

When she offered to care for all unwanted babies, she meant exactly what she said – not just the fit and beautiful ones, but the deformed, the ugly, the retarded. And so at the Shishu Bhavan there are children partially crippled with polio, a small boy with finger-like projections from his shoulders instead of arms, and another boy with no arms at all – both these with handsome alert faces. There was another baby with a huge ugly haemangioma (a collection of blood vessels like a raised strawberry mark) on his upper lip which was being treated by injections with a view to surgery later. In the long stay homes are some of the more afflicted children – spastics in desperate need of physiotherapy, and mental cases, some definitely mad, some severely retarded. There is a boy of eleven or twelve with a sad, beautiful face, who never speaks, but occasionally makes animal-like screams as he goes through a complicated sequence of movements resembling a strange ritual dance.

There are adoption societies which specialise in placing physically

16

handicapped children, and there are many families willing to take them. In these cases, as in all other adoptions, no child leaves until the Missionaries are entirely satisfied that their new family will be a good one. Those with mental handicaps are far less likely to be adopted and may well live out their lives in one of the Missionaries of Charity homes.

When the first Shishu Bhavan was opened in Calcutta, Mother Teresa's work was not so well known, and it was not possible to arrange suitable adoptions for all the abandoned babies. Consequently some of these original babes have been loved, educated and housed by the nuns and brothers. As one older girl said to me, "Normally when you get married a husband has one mother-in-law, but my future husband will have over a thousand! I wonder what he will think of that!"

When a girl and the nuns decide that she is ready for marriage, then a husband is found. In India it is the custom for parents to arrange marriages, and each day in the local papers there are pages of advertisements for suitable brides and grooms. Even Indians who live abroad advertise for a partner from their native land. I met parents who were excitedly sifting through the applications for marriage to their son and daughter – both of whom are consultant surgeons in the United States.

I went to a double wedding. In one case a boy and girl who had grown up in Shishu Bhavan fell in love and a happy match was arranged. The man works as a driver for the Missionaries and a small house was bought for them. The other girl married a young man whose parents had approached the missionaries to see if a bride could be found for their son. The nuns thoroughly vetted his background, found that he was of good character, had a stable job and suitable accommodation, and an introduction was arranged. For some months the couple saw each other, and they decided that they would marry. In the early hours of the wedding day there were groups of people making garlands of flowers and decorating the courtyard with greenery. A table was laid and in the centre was a large oblong cake, beautifully iced with a picture of four people representing the two newly wed couples. At ten in the morning, the girls appeared surrounded by excited "sisters" and nuns. They looked radiant. It had taken two and a half hours for the nuns to dress them in their wedding clothes and to arrange their hair – and the result was dazzling. A young Jesuit priest officiated – it was his first wedding ceremony. Incense and flowers were on the altar, the ceremony was holy, the singing vivacious and there was joy. No ceremony in India is complete without fireworks, and these were to be heard in great abundance.

After a talk with Mother Teresa and her special blessing, they returned to the festivities at Shishu Bhavan. Candy and cakes, Indian sweetmeats, lots of happy laughter and music.

The following afternoon I was amazed to see a beautiful saried figure rush past me. She had come to invite the nuns at Shishu Bhavan to come to tea in their new married home. What better example could there be to show the security and love that these girls have found during their lives with the Missionaries?

3

Abortion

Have you ever been to an abortion clinic? Have you ever delivered an aborted baby and felt the tiny body struggling for life in your hands? Have you ever looked at this dying child, unique gift from God, and tried to comprehend why man can be so inhuman?

Abortion clinics are sad and tense places devoid of all dignity. (In India abortion is legal in the early months of pregnancy – in many countries it is legal up to seven months.) The authorities are still rather ashamed to admit that such places exist and "nursing home" is often the euphemistic name for abortion clinic. This is a world-wide problem.

It is expensive to have an abortion in India, but the pressures are enormous: I was told by a nun who had come from a strict Hindu family, "It is a scandal for any Indian household to have an unmarried mother in the family, and we have to convince these people that they must not force the girl to have an abortion. Perhaps it is not such a shame in Europe, but in India it is an utter disgrace; in fact you could say that the girl was untouchable." Those who wish to get rid of their unborn baby revert first to abortive tablets – or other old-fashioned remedies. When this fails, money is found to visit a clinic, with inevitable hardships. If the abortion takes place during the first three months of pregnancy the mother will go and queue up for a suction operation. In one clinic which I know, there are two delivery beds, and while one woman is undressing and preparing herself, the doctor is performing the five-minute operation on the next bed. At his feet is a large bucket, and into this bucket the babies are dropped. When it is full, the worker empties it. The wash basin and towels are filthy – nothing is sterilised.

The adjoining rooms are filled with beds for girls who are further on in pregnancy. Sometimes they lie two in each iron bed. The room is dirty and dark – a single cot stands at one side to collect the babies which are too strong to die. There are no sheets on the beds, only a rubber covering on the mattress. The blankets are stained. It is silent apart from the breathing of the frightened girls.

The mothers are in labour. They have had an enema, and they have an abortifacient drip inserted into the vagina. Now they wait for the delivery. This is a time for compassion. There is no going back on their decision, and a child will soon be born. There is fear in the mothers' eyes, as they long for understanding. How difficult it can be for many people to understand, to be able to go to these women, to sit on their beds and to hold their hands – and to try and put themselves in their position, which is one of despair. There is a hungry response to affection. I am persuaded that this is a time for silent practical love, for an

awareness of the psychological trauma, of the heartaches. The hope is that through this understanding the mothers will realise that there is forgiveness by society, and thereby be given the strength not to contemplate another abortion in the future.

Mother Teresa has written to all the local nursing homes to say that her Missionaries of Charity will always accept with love any unwanted baby – no matter how tiny or handicapped the child is. "Even if the child dies within minutes, at least it will have died wanted and surrounded by love," say the nuns who receive these babies. It is true that some babies are sent to the Missionaries of Charity by the abortion clinics, but the sisters are under no illusions that the majority are left to die, unless someone – a nun or one of the priests – happens to call in. In other words there has been little change in their attitude towards the sanctity of life.

Letters have also been sent to local gynaecologists, hospitals and nursing homes to say that if an unmarried mother needs help and understanding, she can go to any of the Missionaries of Charity and she will be looked after – free of charge – while she is pregnant and until the child is weaned. In return the mother helps the nuns with the domestic chores. This way her friends or family need not know of her predicament. The girls wish the babies to be adopted and there is a waiting list of would-be adoptive parents.

Just before Mother Teresa went to Oslo to receive her Nobel Prize, she talked to me about abortion. She had been woken by a telephone call early that morning, to be told that an aborted babe had been left on the door-step of the Mother House. She found the child unwashed and wrapped in some rags. She was grateful that it had been brought to her. She said that sometimes there were happy events and that one morning an anguished husband arrived and told her that his wife was about to have an abortion. They were very poor and it was hard to feed their growing daughters. His wife could not face the future, and had insisted that the only solution was to spend the few rupees they had in obtaining an abortion.

The husband was desperate, and came to the Missionaries for help. Mother Teresa saw him and went immediately to the clinic with him. "We found that the wife was already on the table. If we had arrived a minute later, it might have been too late. I talked to her, and told her of the love of God and that she had been given a very precious gift. I told her that we would help her and be with her in times of trial. She listened to me and wept, then she stepped down from the table and the three of us walked out of the clinic." Eventually a full term son was born to a happy family – their first, and very much wanted male child.

4

Nirmal Hriday

The Place of the Pure Heart

Recently, Mother Teresa and some of her Missionaries were walking through the streets in Bombay, when they saw a man lying on the pavement. This is a common sight in India, but this man looked desperately ill, and had in fact been lying where he was for four days. The Missionaries lifted him up to take him to the nearby *Nirmal Hriday* – and he left much of his skin behind. When they arrived at the home for the dying, they cleaned and dressed his wounds, and made him comfortable until he died – uncomplaining, at peace and loved.

It was the horror of such encounters, the lack of caring among the passers-by, that made Mother Teresa decide finally that her vocation was with the poorest of the poor, and she was determined that she would ensure as far as was in her power that no-one died without dignity and love.

The first home for the destitute and dying was at Kalighat in Calcutta. Kali, the goddess of destruction, is the wife of Siva, and according to Hindu mythology first appeared at the place where her temple now stands. It is now one of the most important Hindu shrines. Mother was given the use of the rest home of this temple, and this was turned into Nirmal Hriday, "the place of the pure heart", even though at first there were difficulties and dangers. Eventually one of the priests from the nearby temple was found by Mother lying outside the temple in a pool of his own excreta. He was dying in the last stages of cholera and everyone was afraid to touch him. Mother gently picked him up and carried him into the home and cared for him. Eventually he died happily, surrounded by love. After this the Missionaries were accepted and encouraged to continue their work. The temple to the goddess of destruction is still one of the focal points of Calcutta, but in the same building is the home where the hopeless are given hope, the destitute are given dignity and all are given love.

I am drawn as by a magnet to Kalighat – or rather it is the people who are the magnets. I am constantly aware of their faces, their sunken, pain-ridden, yet joyful eyes, their loneliness, despair and fear. Yet each one knows that he, or she is loved, and they respond in their different ways – dignity is born.

Starvation is the greatest problem, and leads to many diseases and infections. A man arrived with oedema swelling resulting from mal-nutrition – his leg had burst open like a balloon. The brothers removed the filthy rags covering the wound, and as I was watching them I noticed the skin moving. At first I thought it was pus, then we saw the maggots crawling out and falling on the floor as the disinfectant was used. I saw this man on my first day when working at Kalighat, maggots have become a common sight to me now. The brothers dressed his wounds and carried him, as they would carry the child Jesus, to his clean bed where water and food awaited him. On a more cheerful note, I under-stand that maggots keep a wound "clean".

The brothers, like the nuns, come to Kalighat every day except Thursdays. This is a day reserved for the novices, when they carry out all the work in the home, under supervision, as part of their training. One novice, who had been afraid of working at Kalighat with so many dying and diseased people, broke down in the early morning on the first Thursday. Mother Teresa understood the fear and trepidation and said, "I will pray for you when you are there and remember, that when you are with someone who is dying, love and cherish him as you would love and cherish the dying Christ." The novice returned happy and excited. "Mother, Mother, it was wonderful, I have been holding Christ in my arms for four hours." There is no need to worry about this novice any more.

The brothers are remarkable – I cannot praise too highly the tender-ness and care in the way they dressed the wounds of a dying man. His back was raw as the flesh had been torn off when he had been involved with a train accident. One particular young brother novice would spend hours changing the vast expanse of dressings each day, and gently cleaning the wound. He could not speak the same dialect as the dying man, yet there was a deep understanding. I said to the brother that he was achieving a miracle, as the man who had seemed certain to die, was recovering. "No," said the brother, "it is not I who am achieving the miracle, it is God working through me, and while I am working, I am praying to God that He will let me be a channel of His love." He was one with Christ – he loved until it hurt.

"We cannot live without prayer, each morning we become one with Christ when we eat His bread and drink His blood. This is our essential food. We become Christ who loved us so much that He died for us. We

are in Him as He is in us. We pray that in our work we will never let Him down through our own weakness, for He is our strength."

Each Sunday we have Mass at Kalighat – it is a beautiful ceremony conducted by Father Antoine S.J. who is in charge of a student hostel in the slum area and lives in it himself. He speaks in Bengali and English. The altar is the medicine table which is on the platform of the men's ward. Although there are only about six Christian patients at any one time, there is great respect for the service and there is always silence.

One day, Mother Teresa arrived with a hundred novices and professed nuns and brothers to take part in a Mass celebrating the twenty-fifth anniversary of another Jesuit. A feast of a meal for all patients was prepared in the cooking area between the men's and women's wards. A man had just been brought in on the verge of death, and we had to give him an intravenous injection to ease the pain. This involved going up on to the platform in order to get the injection in the middle of the Mass – it was so natural and normal. Then another man, John, called out in anxiety; he was dying of polio. I went and knelt by him as the priest started praying our Lord's prayer. I held John in my arms and prayed, and then I felt someone close by me – it was Mother Teresa – she too had come to help give comfort. The whole essence of Mass came into reality.

During this same Mass there was a commotion outside, with more and more voices making themselves heard. We thought that it was part of a Hindu festival which was in progress, but in fact the crowd was calling for Mother Teresa. She had to go out and gently ask them to be patient until the end of Mass. The love and respect which the Indians have for Mother Teresa and the Missionaries of Charity is all the greater because they do not try to proselytise. Just as the Hindus respected Mother Teresa, she and her Missionaries respect other religions. Those who die in Kalighat are buried according to the faith to which they belonged. God is available to all, and meets every man and woman at death.

Kalighat was the first home – now there are many Nirmal Hridays all over India. The only difference is that the other homes also look after the mentally handicapped, whereas in Calcutta there are special homes for these people.

There is an extraordinary variety of patients. A young lad recovered from meningitis followed by pneumonia. At first he had fits and for days it seemed doubtful that he would last through the following night. However, he eventually responded to treatment and prayer, and at the end of a month was well and happy. Ellen Peterson, who was one of the foreign workers, tended him with great devotion. She fed him through a tube at first and later with a spoon. Her caring love was an important part of his recovery and her understanding.

A lady was brought in by two men who had found her unconscious in the gutter. They said that bandicoots had eaten her head, and certainly there was a wound that exposed a large area of skull. (Bandicoots are cat-sized rats found in India. They are extremely voracious and a danger to any unconscious person on the streets.) She responded rapidly to treatment.

Another woman was brought in by her family, with skin peeling off every part of her body. She lay whimpering on the bed. Sister Luke in her nine years of caring for the dying, had never seen such a severe skin complaint. Each time we took off her blanket, a layer of skin came away. How could a family keep a woman in such a condition? She was sent by ambulance to the infectious diseases hospital, but was returned immediately. Sister Luke insisted on feeding and caring for this poor sad lady herself, for she thought the complaint might have been very infectious – this was typical of her. The woman died a few days later.

A sad example of man's inhumanity to man came in – a beautiful boy of twelve. He was suffering from gonorrhoea and syphilis, and had been used as a prostitute. His widowed mother had forced him to do this, as it was the only way she knew that she and her family could raise money and avoid starvation. He was terrified of injections, and when I gave him his first one he cried. I tried to give him love and comfort, but his eyes remained desperate. He eventually returned to his family.

Working in homes for the dying is not just gentle "do-gooding", it involves the mundane and unpleasant tasks such as changing diarrhoea-soaked sheets of incontinent patients, suffering from one of the many varieties of enteric diseases found in India – such as dysentery, gastroenteritis and typhoid. These sheets are washed next to the mortuary, and dried on the roof. There are no washing machines here, everything has to be done by hand and pounded on stone. Another highly unpleasant job is emptying and washing the sputum pots filled with thick foul catarrh from the T.B. patients. I have never heard anyone complain over doing this task – and it is done continually throughout the day. Nearly everyone has worms, many types. Two women patients were so startled to see such large worms, that they promptly swallowed them again. However the worms have to be cleared so that the feeble bodies can take advantage of the food and vitamins needed to strengthen them. Heads have to be shaved due to lice.

One of the commonest diseases in all age groups is T.B., and T.B. of a degree that is just not seen in Europe these days. It is of course a disease

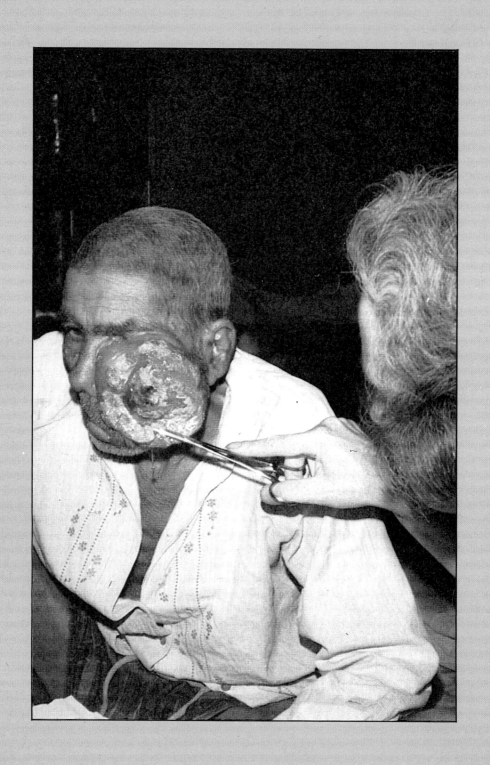

that is easily caught when the body is grossly undernourished, and this semi-starvation prevents healing. There are T.B. hospitals, but most patients are too poor to continue the treatment for long. Even if the treatment is free, the patients have to go back to help finance their families. When they are desperately ill, many come into a home for the dying. Treatment there often improves them enough so that they can be discharged, but to the only home they know – which is on the streets, and from which they will return all too soon back to the home of the dying. Patients who are discharged are provided with clothing, a little money and a blanket in the winter months.

Because of T.B. and starvation, Indians tend to die before reaching the cancer or cardiac age groups. Those who do develop cancer can expect little in the way of treatment, and so the cancer progresses more rapidly and more unpleasantly than in cases seen in the Western world.

Someone brought in a man whom he had found in the gutter. When we turned him over we saw that the whole of the left side of his face had been eaten away with cancer. The wound was crawling with maggots – "large fat white maggots – not the normal thin ones," said Sister. The wound was obviously cancerous with deep growths and tunnels spreading inside his mouth so much that he could not eat or move his jaw. It took three full days to clear the maggots away, because they kept escaping down his throat, yet when they were still crawling over him, he lay quiet. He looked beautiful. His right eye showed no fear – his left had been eaten away by the disease. He was asked how he felt – was there anything to be got to comfort him? "No," he replied, "I am at peace, thank-you."

In a nearby bed was an old man with cancer of the rectum extending to the outside. He insisted on dressing this himself and would walk unsteadily to the toilet to do this. However, he allowed us to deal with a large ulcerated secondary deposit in his right groin – a growth that burrowed daily nearer to the main artery in his leg. He had pain, but after being given quite simple pain-killers would say with a tender smile, "Thank-you, the pain is much less now." Both these sufferers have died now. They taught us all a great deal – an understanding of life and the meaning of death.

I went to a lady one morning – she was on her hands and knees as the pain caused through her hip sarcoma was so great that she could not lie down on her back. She was desperately anaemic and jaundiced. We gave her an analgesic, and all I could do was to squat at the end of the bed and stroke her head which I held to me. We stayed thus for half an hour, then she spoke and indicated that she wanted me to find someone to translate. I called over an elderly ayah (a patient who had looked

after as a nanny the children of twenty British families), expecting to hear that the woman wanted further relief – but all she had said was, "Thank-you for your love." I felt very small and asked the ayah to thank her for allowing me to help – for I was being given a far greater revelation of the Gospel. How easy it is to love the poor, destitute and dying – how difficult it is to do the same to the spoilt and selfish who may really need it more.

In one home there is a woman aged about sixty, who was found in the forest at the foot of the Himalayas, some years ago. She was found by a hunter and she was "travelling" on her hands and feet. It was thought that she had been brought up by the bears that were with her. She was unable to walk, and had to be taught by the nuns to go on her "hind" legs. Even now she walks with her feet turned in. It took a long time before her stomach could adjust to human food, and for a long time she would only eat her food off the ground. She is a delight and full of fun, but she cannot hear or make any noise. It is believed that her vocal cords have dried up due to lack of use. She loves being massaged from under her arm to her hips. Is this a memory of the bears caressing and licking her?

There are many long-term patients, such as a very brave man who has lost both legs above the knee through an accident, yet can always be cheerful. There is another who is completely paralysed from the waist down, due to another accident. He is young, tall and good-looking. He never complains.

There are a number of mentally handicapped people at Nirmal Hriday. One of my greatest joys is to find how much I have learnt from them. The total love which is given by the Missionaries, penetrates to all, and there is great tenderness between the patients. Hours will be spent by one mental patient feeding another who is worse than himself – perhaps because the other is paralysed – then clearing up the spilt food from his clothes, washing his face, and eventually bringing him the urine bottle to make him comfortable. There is utter devotion and love which knows no embarrassment.

Many reporters have interviewed Mother, particularly after she received the Nobel Prize. I have been involved with both Americans and Canadians. Neither group had adapted themselves psychologically to the poverty and despair of Calcutta. Both groups came for a week, and both had to leave after two days. I said, "Surely you must have experienced slum life and the degredation that it entails in previous commissions?"

"We have been to the slums of Mexico and Peru," they replied, "and even covered refugees fleeing in war, but there is nothing to compare

31

with Calcutta – there is no escape route here." When they returned to their luxury hotel after visiting Kalighat, they collapsed – some in tears – and immediately made arrangements to leave.

"The nuns and brothers are all angels," said a Canadian reporter.

"We do it all for Jesus," is the Missionaries' reply.

On the one day when I was feeling overwhelmed at the seeming impossibility of ever producing any permanent improvement, I went to the Chapel at the Mother House. Mother saw me and beckoned. I said, "What we do seems no more than a drop in the ocean, it does not seem to make any difference." Mother put her arm round my shoulder. "The ocean is made of drops," she said. That was all that I needed.

Mother has an answer to everything. Choosing superiors is one of her most important problems. One superior who was due to be transferred to a new house, felt that she would like to step down in favour of someone else. When she went to talk to Mother about this, she asked a friend to pray for her – "No," said the friend, "I never pray against certainties." Mother dealt with the situation in her usual direct manner (I know of no-one who goes more directly to the heart of any problem!): "Hold my hand," she said, "now look at me and repeat after me six times, 'I will continue to be a good superior!' " There was no further protest; what she needed was Mother's reassurance.

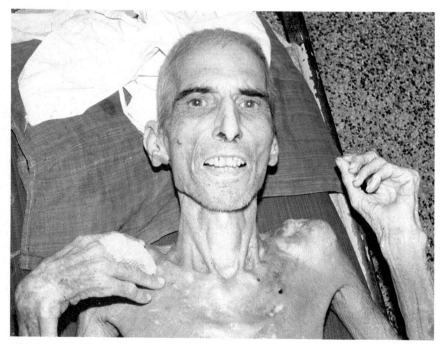

5

Leprosy

I have frequently heard it said that leprosy is on the decrease. Most people in this country, if they think about leprosy victims at all, think about them as people in the Bible who featured in various miraculous healings. In other countries, however, leprosy victims exist now. In India, there are about three and a half million known cases.

It starts so simply – just a small patch of skin that looks different from the rest – but it may progress to the stage where fingers and toes are lost and muscles are paralysed because of damage to the nerves. Leprosy particularly affects the nerves that transmit feelings of pain and excessive heat and cold, so that patients are often unaware of the danger that threatens them.

Leprosy involves the same sort of social rejection that T.B. used to in the West. Mother Teresa tells the story of the businessman who developed the first signs. He told his wife, who said, "We have two daughters. If this is known, they will never get husbands. You must leave home." He left, could not get work because of his disease, and was eventually found by some Missionaries of Charity in the slums on the verge of suicide. Today, with the disease arrested, he is one of Mother's most able helpers.

At the foothills of the Himalayas is a small town about two hundred miles north-east of Delhi. I visited a leprosy colony run by an elderly German nurse, and supervised by a Franciscan priest. This was a local organisation, with no connection with Mother Teresa and her Missionaries of Charity, and it reminded me that, happily, many people and organisations are working in India – though still nowhere near enough for all the needs. In common with other leprosy settlements we had seen, these patients were occupied with weaving, but to a very professional standard. They did everything from spinning the thread and dyeing it, to turning the finished cloth into clothing, table cloths, blankets and so on. Their standards were so high that their products were sent by air all over the world. They worked without patterns –

their own natural sense of colour and form was enough. It was very sad to see their best designer teaching a beautiful young woman in the early stages of the disease – the designer himself had lost his fingers in a fire which he had never felt.

Leprosy patients feel their rejection keenly, and in return they are often aggressive. As the result of a bitter disagreement, this leprosy colony recently had a split, and about one hundred and forty of them had left to be looked after by three brothers from the Missionaries of Charity. They were all young men, and they were the only ones of their order for miles around. After the busy Mother House in Calcutta, they must at times have felt very isolated. In addition to these patients whom they had "acquired", they were working among the destitute and dying, and trying also to do some infant teaching in the poorest areas of the town.

As yet, the brothers have no building of their own. They rent a few rooms in a house, but they had managed to find room for a tiny Chapel and a dispensary in addition to their living quarters. As is the case with all the houses where the nuns and brothers live, this one was spotlessly clean. They often have to comfort and treat people as they lie in the street for they have nowhere to take them. I was able to give them some drugs bought with money given to me by friends in Britain and to leave them some money to buy more for themselves. When I arrived unexpectedly at Dehra Dun and brought a good supply of antibiotics and analgesics donated by British friends, the brothers exclaimed, "Now we have enough for at least three months." It was wonderful to give them money to provide for food and further medicines. It was wonderful to see their faces. They do not worry about the future, for they have faith in God's generosity, and I doubt if they ever worry about anything in the way we do. They remain gentle and loving and deeply happy. Their first action when they received the money, was to buy a little extra food so that we could all share a meal together. They had no money of their own for hospitality – or for anything beyond bare essentials. That simple meal was a feast.

After I returned to England one of them wrote:

> I am glad to remember the day when we met each other after the Holy Mass at St. Francis' Church. That day was a real God's grace to us because there was no money at all in our house. I trust more in Christ because I was empty-handed but He gave me a sum of money which I received from you. It was a real blessing day of God.

People's gifts, often anonymous, also provided 12,000 hypodermic needles. When the sisters saw them, it seemed like a miracle. Disposable needles are used sometimes thirty or more times – they are treated like gold. 12,000 needles do not last long in the 145 homes which are dotted about India – particularly as those used on leprosy patients can only be used once. Needles and syringes are frequently sent, but although many syringes arrive, it is rare to find the needles – they vanish on the journey.

Melolin dressings are expensive, and yet vital in a country where so many suffer from starvation, which leads to all types of illness including problems of healing. Legs may swell with oedema, and then the skin bursts to leave a large ulcer. Many other patients have large areas where skin and subcutaneous tissue has been lost due to burns or infection. The skin is very fragile, and ordinary dressings are difficult to change when soaked with blood or pus, but with Melolin, changing dressings becomes painless. The patients' fears are minimised, and excitement grows when they realise that their bodies can cope with healing. Vitamins are another healing agent, building a worn, concentration-camp type body into a human being again – a human being with dignity.

Wherever they work, the Missionaries of Charity are only too well aware of the sight of beggars with leprosy, as they thrust forward their deformed and stunted hands for alms. They have built, and are continuing to build villages for leprosy patients. My first visit was to Titagarh, a suburb of Calcutta. The leprosy rehabilitation centre is run by seven brothers. This is housed in buildings made mostly by the patients themselves, and is on both sides of the railway line, immediately next to the track. Between the buildings and the railway station is a dung brick centre, where numerous women and children shape bricks by hand from moist cow dung, and leave them to dry in the sun.

Brother Christo Das is the superior in the home. That morning I found him giving his final medical lecture of a course to six nuns. This was particularly interesting as he was giving a résumé of his previous lectures over the past few months. These nuns would then be sent to various houses in India, and it would be their responsibility to set up centres for leprosy sufferers in their area. The girls look very young, but they have been picked to take the responsibility and they responded joyfully and willingly. Certainly they had done their homework and enthusiastically answered all the questions put to them – they had made copious notes which would, no doubt, be referred to in the future.

He has specialised in the treatment of leprosy. He is revered throughout India, and other brothers and nuns in charge of leprosy settlements will state with pride that they have been trained by him. He is a humble man. "The leprosy sufferers have a very difficult time, their treatment is long and great patience is required. There are many psychological problems which they have to overcome. We are very grateful to be able

to help them with their illness, but of course they give us far more than we can ever give them."

We went on a tour of the out-patients, dressing rooms, and to the wards where the infectious patients were isolated. Seventy per cent of patients are non infectious, but some of these too, need in-patient treatment because they are so dreadfully mutilated by the disease.

We were all shown a man with, literally, half his foot missing and the metatarsal bones sticking out into the air. He had arrived that morning.

Healthy looking young men have to queue up each week to have treatment due to having a small area of infected skin. Others lay on beds with the remains of their infected limbs covered with bandages. Leprosy first attacks the skin, peripheral nerves and lymph nodes. Later, if untreated, it attacks all the organs, but the skin lesions, missing fingers and toes result from injuries due to the lack of sensation.

However, there are many sufferers who may be badly deformed, yet are under treatment, and desperately need to be rehabilitated. They were encouraged to build large mill sheds, and here men and women were briskly weaving material for shirts, sheets, *lungis* (men's wear), bandages etc., all of which will be used at Missionaries of Charity homes.

The first large village for leprosy patients was built at Shantinagar – "the place of peace" – which is two hundred miles away, and takes five hours to reach from Howrah station. Sister Francis Xavier has performed a miracle in transforming the barren desert into something beautiful for God – and something beautiful for leprosy sufferers, for it is here that they have their own place, where they can live and work in peace and die with dignity.

Sister Francis Xavier is a doctor and now through her encouragement further miracles are performed in the operating theatres which have been built at this centre. Limbs which have suffered through leprosy can sometimes be made whole in the sense that they become functional and useful. Orthopaedic surgery is giving new hope to many.

There is another very large centre being built outside Delhi. Here, as at Shantinagar, land has been given by the Indian government. Mother Teresa's policy is always to involve the local people, so that they become aware of their responsibilities. Again the barren land will bloom with nature, houses are being built for men and women suffering from this dreaded disease, and the rehabilitation centre will be enlarged. Leprosy sufferers in the villages had been stripped of their pride and self-respect before they came. It is essential that they come to realise that through their efforts beauty can be made, and both pride and self-respect restored.

40

6

Other Works

In all parts of the world, people know something about Mother Teresa's main work among abandoned children and in her homes for the destitute and dying. There are other important activities of the Missionaries which are not so well known.

One of these activities is cooking and distributing food to the starving. Once again the start of this work was in Calcutta. At Shishu Bhavan every night, fires are lit in the courtyard. The enormous cooking vessels bubble with rice, curry and dhal, and vast containers are filled to the brim throughout the night in preparation for the influx next morning of the poorest of the poor. Seven thousand people are fed each day from this one place. A careful check has to be kept so that people do not return to the queue and present their pots for a second filling. This pattern is carried out in one way or another at all the homes throughout the world.

Another activity is medical clinics. There are some qualified doctors among the Missionaries, and many with some form of medical training. This enables them to operate daily clinics providing free simple medicines which have been donated from many countries. This is a far cry from the early days when Mother Teresa had no medicines freely available, and she sometimes had to take the relatives of very ill people to chemists' shops in the wealthier part of Calcutta. She would sit there until the pharmacist dispensed the urgently required medicines without cost. The very sick are admitted to a home or a hospital bed found when necessary – the Missionaries sometimes having to provide money to pay the patients' bill.

There are also family planning clinics. I opened, with some surprise a box of thermometers which had been sent out by Sister Marie Celine in London. Mother exclaimed, "Ah, for my family planning clinic!"

Stations are areas of high activity in India, and outside many a station you may come across a group of nuns or brothers holding clinics for medicines or treatment clinics for lepers. There are also mobile clinics which go out into the villages.

There are thousands of children who will never enter a school building in India. A few fortunate ones will be given the rudiments of education by the brothers and sisters. "However poor and ill-equipped our makeshift schools may be," said one young brother, "at least we keep the children off the streets, and give them friendship and food." He also said that it is often through the children that they learn which families are in greatest need.

Visiting families is another important work for the Missionaries. There are many Christian families, and where they are welcomed, the Missionaries are always ready to teach catechetics – the basics of the Christian faith. Mother will say that this is one of the most important parts of their apostolate.

One effect of the increasing fame of the Missionaries of Charity has been to attract helpers from every race. There are men and women of all ages who pay their own fares and find their own accommodation and food. They come for a day – or six months – and most are willing to do whatever is necessary. Not surprisingly, the vast majority go to Calcutta, but as Mother Teresa herself constantly points out, there are needs in her other houses in India and all over the world. In fact it is probably true to say that wherever there is a house belonging to the Missionaries, there is a need for help.

Those who go to work, should be prepared to "give their all", but in the end they will find they have gained more than they gave. The experience gained from working in India must be brought to bear on problems elsewhere – not only among the sick and dying, but among the lonely, who may be the richest of all materially.

7

Love Until It Hurts

Mother Teresa never writes articles, but she makes speeches. This is a summary made of a recent speech she gave in the packed Cathedral at Delhi.

Hail Mary full of grace, the Lord is with thee. Blessed art thou among women, and blessed is the fruit of thy womb, Jesus. Holy Mary, Mother of God, pray for us sinners now and at the hour of our death.

God so loved the world that He gave us His only begotten Son. What greater gift could be given?

Mary was free from sin – she was pure and was chosen by God to be the mother of His babe. When Mary was pregnant, she visited her cousin Elizabeth and as they greeted each other the babe in Elizabeth's womb leapt for joy when confronted with Mary's divine Child.

Is that not marvellous? That an unborn child should leap for joy when in the presence of the divine Child?

Are we not all divine? Are we not all made for a higher life?

When a child in the womb is killed, are we not crucifying Christ?

When a mother decides to have an abortion, when a father agrees to do away with his unwanted, unborn child, when a doctor aborts a babe, then each one is crucifying the divine Child of God.

Christ suffered. He experienced poverty. He was the object of jealousy. He was derided, ridiculed and humiliated. He knew torture and He was then crucified.

Christ also knew love, kindness, compassion and sympathy. He loved until it hurt. He understood utter loneliness and despair, yet He loved until it hurt.

He loved us so much – He was hurt so much through His love that He became the bread of life, and made Himself available for us all to take – even for a little child to take.

When we take this bread of life we have Christ in us – we too have God's divine Son. We too are sons of God, and we are in Christ as He is in us.

Do you know of the houses that are run by the Missionaries of Charity? There are now over a hundred and forty in India alone.

In Calcutta, there is a Hindu temple to Kali at Kalighat; we were given the guest house belonging to this temple for the care of those who were dying in poverty.

Thirty-nine thousand patients have been brought to Kalighat, and of these nineteen thousand have died, yet they never complain, they never die in despair, for they are given love. It is we who say "thank-you" to them for allowing us the privilege of serving them.

I brought in a lady from the streets – there were maggots crawling out of her wounds. These wounds were washed and she lay dying. What would I have done if I had been that woman? I would have tried to attract attention, but all she said was "thank-you". I learnt love and humility from her.

There was a Hindu woman who had eight children and no money to buy food. I took rice and curry to the family. The mother divided the

food into half, and took a half share to a Muslim woman who also had starving children. "Their need is as great as ours," said the Hindu woman. I was not surprised that she had shared her food, but I was surprised that the Hindu woman *knew*.

Do we know our neighbour's needs in this pluralistic society? Or are we kept at home by television?

Our order of Missionaries of Charity have a home in New York. One day they were called to go to a flat where a number of milk bottles stood outside the door. Inside the flat they found a dead woman. No-one knew her name – they only knew the milk which she had ordered.

Love begins at home – in the family – with your neighbours. "Love one another as I have loved you," said our Lord.

Are we helping the poor, the lonely, the oppressed?

People want to see Christ in others. Therefore, we must love Christ with undivided love until it hurts. It must be a total surrender, a total conviction that nothing separates us from the love of Christ. We belong to Christ.

The Missionaries of Charity choose to live in poverty in order to help those who are poor. Thus the fourth vow which each Missionary takes is to dedicate his or her life in giving themselves wholeheartedly and totally to the poorest of the poor.

In Calcutta our sisters and brothers feed seven thousand people daily. One day there was no money to buy any rice. No one knew how the food would be provided, but they had faith, and without warning several truck loads of bread arrived from a cancelled schools' function. The hungry and destitute had never eaten so much bread.

Recently, during a period of sugar rationing, a child arrived clutching a small bag of sugar. "I do not need this, please take it to give to the poor," he said. He had saved his own ration for four days.

There is so much love in us all, but we are often too shy to express our love and we keep it bottled up inside us. We must learn to love, to love until it hurts and we will then know how to accept love.

We must be a channel of peace.

We must love until it hurts.

We must be Christ.

We must not be afraid to show our love.

India is recognising the works of love, so too is the world. The Nobel Prize was awarded for love – is this not wonderful? If you love, then there is peace in your soul and joy in your heart.

Love God, love God in the womb. Love God in the unborn Child. Love God in the family. Love God in your neighbour. Love until it hurts.

8

Joy

True joy is one of the greatest gifts of life, it blossoms from within and is the result of love, love which matures then bursts open for all to see. It is the soul laid bare. Joy is not confined to the Religious or "do-gooder" (who may often be so intense that they cannot experience joy), but it comes to those who in a sense forget themselves and become totally aware of the other. Mother says that what we actually do makes no difference but how much love, honesty and faith are put into doing it.

Mother understands joy, and throughout their training she has always led her novices towards sharing in this understanding by becoming fully aware of God's gift to the world. The Missionaries have this joy in all the work they do – no matter how apparently degrading that work. It has nothing to do with material possessions. It is one of the fruits of the Spirit. Mother is also aware that another of the fruits is a sense of humour which in turn often makes joy possible – and I am sure St. Paul would agree!

The brothers and sisters radiate joy. It is not only the poor and the destitute who are Christ, but all people. One day I was delayed by traffic and arrived unexpectedly at a home of the brothers at the awkward hour of two p.m. I was immediately given lunch, and all the brothers came into the refectory to welcome and talk to me. They had been up since four thirty a.m., and would not rest again until nine p.m., yet they greeted me and welcomed me into their family with joy. We went to the Chapel and prayed silently, then while I ate some lunch they talked of their work – of the leprosy clinics which they run, of the homes for leprosy sufferers in their last stage of illness, of the abandoned boys that were in their charge, of the schools they organised in the streets of the slums and of the home which we were in for the destitute and dying. Their work was not a burden to them, it was a joyful experience. I had a tour round their spotlessly clean wards and saw the faces of the men on the verge of death shine when they saw and spoke to the brothers. I saw the children – some were patients, others were sons of patients – and the

49

joy of the brothers had penetrated the children whose out-stretched hands they held. The sick were comforted. After our tour, we returned to the Chapel to thank God for His love.

Another day I was with nuns feeding premature babies. What joy it is when an aborted baby gains in strength and is able to transfer from an intravenous drip to milk being fed through a dropper and then to a babies' bottle. A nun was happily feeding two babies on her knee, when she started laughing. I turned and saw that one of these little ones had a loose nappy and Sister Teresina's apron and sari were thoroughly soaked. "In this ward we are allowed to have an extra sari and habit – it is often needed," she said to a bemused bishop who was watching.

A Jesuit celebrated his Silver Jubilee with a Mass at Mother House. Flowers filled every corner of the Chapel and courtyard. After Mass a breakfast was prepared, but first he wanted to say thank-you to all the nuns and novices who had prayed with him and who had helped to make his day such a happy one. He stood by Mother in the courtyard with garlands round his neck. Every time he finished his sentence, the large dog belonging to the novices answered by barking. Soon we were all reduced to helpless laughter. "Even the dog is sharing our joy," said the Jesuit. A speech that no-one will forget.

After Mother had been awarded the highest prize India could give her, the Jewel of India, she made several speeches in Delhi. Some groups of people called at the home for the dying, Nirmal Hriday, and asked if they could feed the hundred and forty patients. Even in Delhi these people had not heard of Nirmal Hriday which had just celebrated its fifteenth anniversary. A few days later a group of men arrived with large pots to cook the Sunday lunch, and when all was ready they took the food round to each patient. "It is we who have received the joy," they said, "we will do this each month."

A girl, aged about eight, came one morning with a small tin bowl. She saw a sister and gave the bowl to her. "This is my food for the day, I want to give it to someone in need." It was given with joy. This child had just heard of Nirmal Hriday and she had given what she could.

Sister Shirley has a ward of children of all ages. Not all are abandoned, some are brought to her by distraught parents who cannot afford medicines or hospital treatment. One baby I saw appeared to be five or six months old: she was in fact at least three years old as she had her milk molars. Her appearance was due to starvation. In addition she was desperately ill and for three nights Sister Shirley stayed beside the cot praying and caring for her. The child died surrounded by love. "It gives me great joy in my sorrow, to have been able to give my love and prayer to this little one – it was a privilege for me."

Material goods must be given with joy. It was suggested that one day a year is set aside for flag day in order to raise money for the Missionaries' work. "No," said Mother, "I do not want people to be forced to give money – it must come with joy from the heart. I would far rather that the person who would contribute automatically when a collecting box is held out to him, gives time to reflect what the collection is about, and thinks if there is anyone in his office or at home who may be in need, and does something about it." She is quite right, how much greater the gift is if it comes joyfully from the heart, and the giver thereby knows the joy of sharing, the joy of giving, the joy of awareness and love.

This, Mother says, is why the work of the Missionaries is so beautiful. They are contemplatives rather than social workers. "The spirit of the congregation is total surrender to God, loving trust in our superiors, and cheerfulness because without joy there is no love, and love without joy is not true love." They follow the teachings of Christ when He said, "I was hungry and you gave me food, I was thirsty and you gave me drink, I was a stranger and you welcomed me, I was naked and you clothed me, I was sick and you visited me, I was in prison and you came to me." Because they really see Christ in all these people – then that is contemplation. Touching Christ in the destitute is joy, is real, is loving and is beautiful. The poor do not need negative pity, they need compassion and love and to know that they are loveable and great people. Then they too can accept the love which is given with joy.

9

All That I Have

This has been a book on love, on the heartaches and suffering experienced by everyone in all parts of the world. Poverty is real, and if we are honest with ourselves we can each say that we are one with the poorest of the poor. We all want to love, but by giving love, we are embarrassed and afraid that we might be rejected. We all need to receive love, yet many of us cannot accept love when it is freely given. Perhaps we can only give our greatest gift once we acknowledge our instinctive fear – "I give you myself; if you reject it, it is all that I have."

I also have been devoid of love for much of my life. I had no childhood family in the conventional sense. I had no base, but somewhere along the line I was given a faith. In desperation at the age of four I held a spiritual hand, and with a mature, yet childlike simplicity came the certain knowledge that God is there, and that He is in me, as I am in Him. Then I was never alone.

There is no hypocrisy in God. That is the beauty. I am frightened of hypocrisy, of having a double standard in life. I cannot cope with arguments and outwardly I accepted this way of life in our self-sufficient society. I saw how many people were strained and unhappy, that there was an invisible wall behind which they lived and played their games. Some could not admit to themselves their failure to understand the real love which we need in order to live our lives to the full. They become obsessed with themselves and with others. The psychologists write volumes on the theories of Jung and Freud. Sex is in – and love considered rare. The consequences were obvious – do what you like when you like, life is too short – so enjoy it. Think only of the present, and most important of all, think only of yourself. The state is on our side – "they" will provide.

Mother Teresa came over to England some years ago at Christmas time, and said, "I am amongst middle-class people who seem to be unhappy and have no aim in life – why is this?" The Simon Community was asked to show her London by night, and a tour was arranged visiting Waterloo station with the alcoholics, the Thames embankment with the "down and outs", and Picadilly Circus where the drug addicts queued at the all-night chemist. They were waiting for midnight when their prescriptions became valid and they could get their next day's supply of drugs. Eventually they came to the methylated spirit drinkers huddled round an open fire at the old Covent Garden. They had gone there for companionship as the fruit stalls were open all night. Then a young man with long hair came to the fire – he was high on drugs. He had a handful of barbiturates and swallowed them. The Simon Community took him to hospital. His pulse was weak, and he died with his pockets half-full of old syringes and needles. He was already frightened and alone before he reached the ultimate loneliness of the mortuary. One evening with the Simon Community had given Mother her answer, and today we are privileged to have three houses in London and one in Liverpool run by the Missionaries of Charity.

The Missionaries come from all over the world. They could be you and me, they are universal in every sense of the word. Men and women came originally to Calcutta and from there have gone out to open houses in all parts of the world. But they are all one in their love. Mother Teresa's "awareness of life" has penetrated each soul, and sparked the joy of bringing understanding and love. Other people of *all* faiths all over the world have travelled the same road. When we read the prayers of Cardinal Newman and St. Francis, when we learn to give ourselves without restraint, when we come to terms with ourselves, then we too begin to live.

I was thirsty for knowledge and I desperately wanted to return to the continent of my birth. I knew that in India there would be no need to live behind my wall, that I could be reborn and be educated anew. I went unannounced to Sister Marie Celine who runs the Mother House in London and arrived during Mass. Immediately I was part of the family of aspirants and nuns. In the poverty of that home, I knew it *was* home. In her humility and self-sacrifice I knew that I had found the answer I had been searching for. Last Christmas, after my return from Calcutta, we took them some food and later had a letter which said:

> . . . a very special thanks to you for your kindness at Christmas for bringing us all those lovely goodies. As we had not prepared anything for ourselves, your gift was truly welcome. God bless you for your generosity.

These Indian nuns had given all they had to the English down-and-outs.

At this first visit, Sister Marie Celine said, "There is going to be a sexennial General Meeting for the Order in October. The older nuns will be very busy, and a lot will be on retreat. If you have worked with the dying, please arrange to go to Calcutta then – you will be needed." I muttered something about finding the money for the fare. "It will come, Daphne, if God wants you to go – you will be given the ticket." The following week, quite unexpectedly, I was given the ticket.

I had been in Calcutta for only a few minutes when I became totally immersed in the land and the people. I reverted at once to my early childhood, and to the memory of the sights and smells, the heat and chaos. When I was confronted with the diseases of the Eastern world, the starved and worn bodies, I felt no surprise. There was no time for horror – Christ was there and was in need. I was given so much by these poorest of the poor. I became "aware", and yet thirsty for an increased depth of understanding. My thirst is slowly being quenched. I have been asked what the overall effect has been on me. I cannot answer fully, but I begin to find it easy to give what I have and not fear rejection.

I have found the paradox that if I love until it hurts, then there is no hurt, but only more love. As I held and fed the morsel of life that was an aborted baby, as I held the hand of a man dying from cancer and felt his trust and gratitude, I could see, feel and touch God's love which has existed from the beginning. The Kingdom of God, I realised, is within reach of everyone, and is to be found in the love we bear one another.

"Lord, make us worthy to serve our fellow-men . . ."

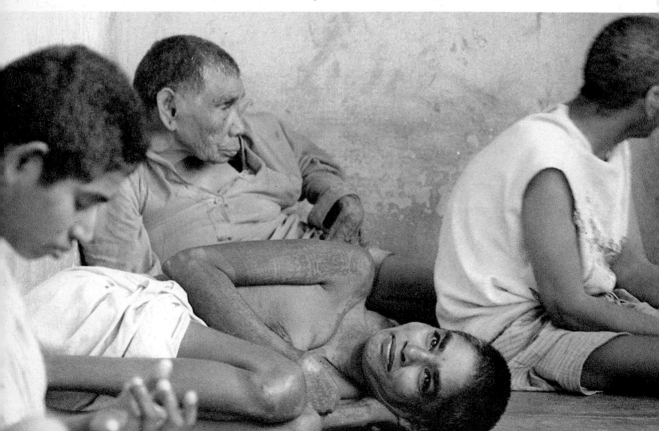

Prayers from the
Missionaries of Charity

These pictures show moments in the lives of
some of Mother Teresa's nuns and brothers-
who are the Missionaries of Charity.

Together with the pictures are some of the
daily prayers used by all the community.

The world has recognised the service of the
Missionaries of Charity in radiating God
to the poorest of the poor by awarding the
Nobel Peace Prize to Mother Teresa who
inspires us all.

Prayer for Peace

Lord, make me a channel of your peace,
that where there is hatred,
       I may bring love:
where there is wrong,
       I may bring the spirit of forgiveness:
where there is discord,
       I may bring harmony:
where there is error,
       I may bring truth:
where there is doubt,
       I may bring faith:
where there is despair,
       I may bring hope
where there are shadows,
       I may bring light:
where there is sadness,
       I may bring joy:
Lord, grant I may seek rather
       to comfort than to be comforted;
       to understand than to be understood;
       to love than to be loved;
for it is by forgetting self
       that one finds,
it is by forgiving
       that one is forgiven,
it is by dying
       that one awakens to eternal life.

AMEN
after St. Francis

Prayer for Peace

Lord, make me a channel of your peace,
that where there is hatred,
   I may bring love:
where there is wrong,
   I may bring the spirit of forgiveness:
where there is discord,
   I may bring harmony:
where there is error,
   I may bring truth:

where there is doubt,
              I may bring faith:
where there is despair,
              I may bring hope
where there are shadows,
              I may bring light:
where there is sadness,
              I may bring joy:

Lord, grant I may seek rather
          to comfort than to be comforted;
          to understand than to be understood;
          to love than to be loved;
for it is by forgetting self
          that one finds,
it is by forgiving
          that one is forgiven,
it is by dying
          that one awakens to eternal life.

AMEN
after St. Francis

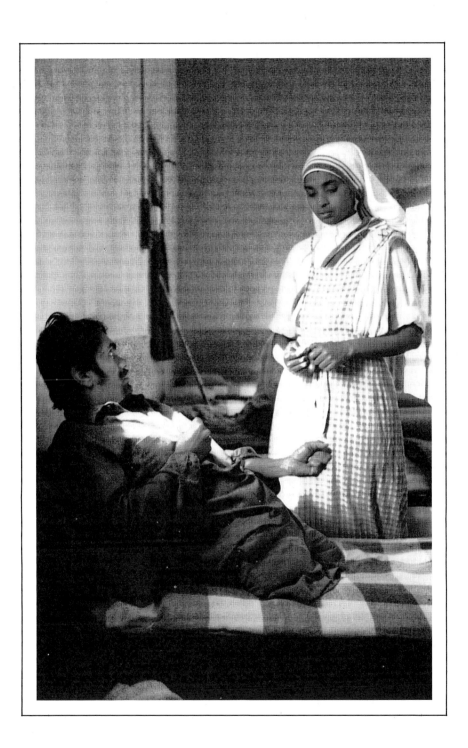

Make us worthy, Lord, to serve our
fellow men throughout the world
who live and die in poverty and
hunger. Give them through our
hands, this day their daily bread,
and by our understanding love,
give peace and joy.
AMEN
Prayer of Pope Paul VI

Radiating Christ

Dear Jesus, help us to spread your fragrance everywhere we go.
Flood our souls with your spirit and life.
Penetrate and possess our whole being so utterly that our
     lives may only be a radiance of yours.
Shine through us, and be so in us, that every soul we come
     in contact with may feel your presence in our soul.
Let them look up and see no longer us but only Jesus!
Stay with us, and then we shall begin to shine as you shine;
so to shine as to be a light to others; the light O Jesus,
     will be all from you, none of it will be ours;
it will be you, shining on others through us.
Let us thus praise you in the way you love best by
     shining on those around us.
Let us preach you without preaching, not by words
     but by our example, by the catching force, the
     sympathetic influence of what we do.
the evident fullness of the love our hearts bear to you.

AMEN
Cardinal Newman

Dear Jesus
    help us to spread your fragrance
        everywhere we go

Flood our souls with your spirit and life

Penetrate and possess our whole being

so utterly,

that our lives may only be a radiance of yours.

Shine through us

and be so in us,
    that every soul we come in contact with
    may feel your presence in our soul.

Let them look up
and see no longer us but only Jesus!

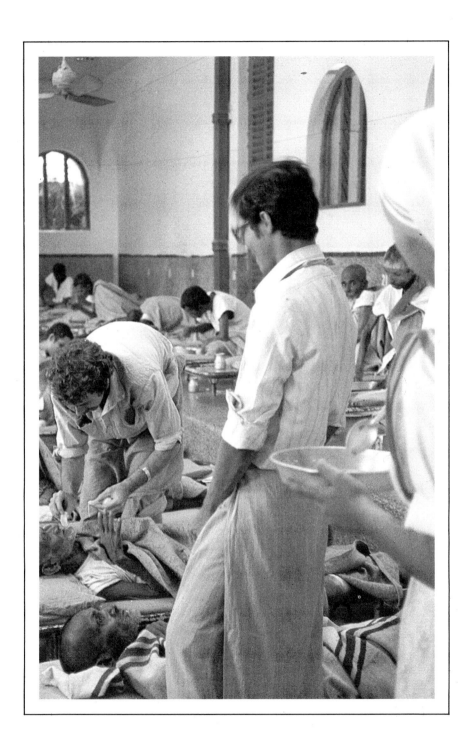

Stay with us
    and then we shall begin to shine
        as you shine;

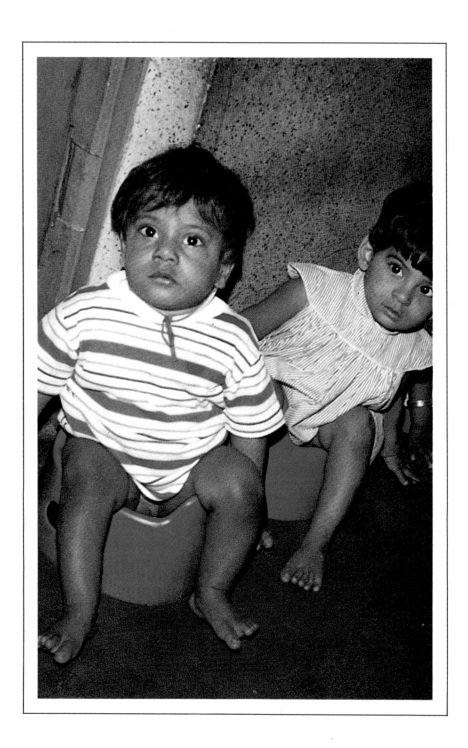

so to shine
   as to be a light to others;

the light O Jesus,
   will be all from you
   none of it will be ours;

it will be you,
   shining on others through us.

Let us thus praise you
      in the way you love best

by shining on those around us.

Let us preach you without preaching,
not by words but by our example,

by the catching force,
  the sympathetic influence of what we do,

the evident fullness
of the love our hearts bear to you.

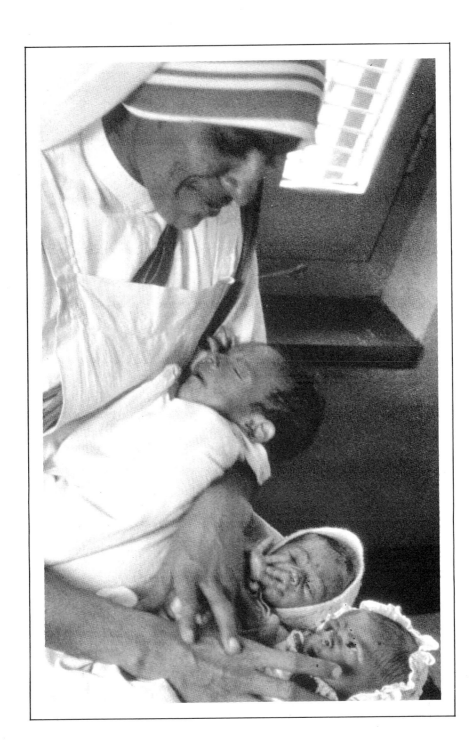

God is Love—and He loves
You and Me. Let us love
Others as He loves us

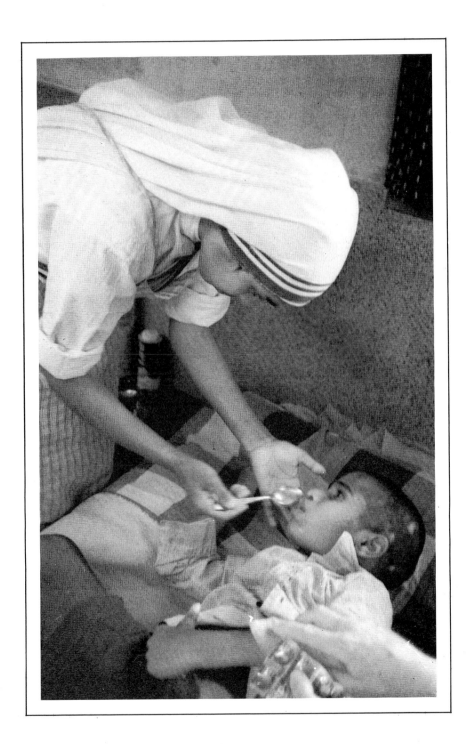

AMEN

If anyone is more aware of God or his neighbour through this
book, then Edward England is responsible. He persuaded me
to put pen to paper.

The Missionaries of Charity provided the inspiration for this book.
It is hoped that others will be helped by it.

British Library Cataloguing in Publication Data
Rae, Daphne
Love until it hurts.
1. Missionaries of Charity
2. Teresa, *Mother*
266:2'0924

ISBN 0 340 26311 3

Phototypeset in Linotron 202 Sabon by Western Printing Services Ltd, Bristol. Book design by
Sharyn Troughton. All photographs have been taken by volunteers working with the
Missionaries of Charity. Printed in Great Britain for Hodder and Stoughton Limited,
Mill Road, Dunton Green, Sevenoaks, Kent by Hazell, Watson & Viney.